ANGLICAN FOUNDATIONS SERIES 08

# TILL DEATH US DO PART

*"The Solemnization of Matrimony"*
*in the Book of Common Prayer*

BY SIMON VIBERT

The Latimer Trust

Till Death Us Do Part: "The Solemnization of Matrimony" in the Book of Common Prayer © Simon Vibert 2014

ISBN 978-1-906327-26-2

Cover photo: © Alexandr Vasilyev- fotolia.com

Scripture quotations are from THE HOLY BIBLE, NEW INTERNATIONAL VERSION®, NIV® Copyright © 1973, 1978, 1984, 2011 by Biblica, Inc.® Used by permission. All rights reserved worldwide.

Published by the Latimer Trust October 2014

The Latimer Trust (formerly Latimer House, Oxford) is a conservative Evangelical research organisation within the Church of England, whose main aim is to promote the history and theology of Anglicanism as understood by those in the Reformed tradition. Interested readers are welcome to consult its website for further details of its many activities.

The Latimer Trust
London N14 4PS UK
Registered Charity: 1084337
Company Number: 4104465
Web: www.latimertrust.org
E-mail: administrator@latimertrust.org

Views expressed in works published by The Latimer Trust are those of the authors and do not necessarily represent the official position of The Latimer Trust.

# Foreword to the Anglican Foundations Series

The recent celebration of the 350th anniversary of the 1662 *Book of Common Prayer* has helped to stimulate a renewed interest in its teaching and fundamental contribution to Anglican identity. Archbishop Cranmer and others involved in the English Reformation knew well that the content and shape of the services set out in the Prayer Book were vital ways of teaching congregations biblical truth and the principles of the Christian gospel. This basic idea of *'lex orandi, lex credendi'* is extremely important. For good or ill, the content and shape of our meetings as Christians is highly influential in shaping our practice in following the Lord Jesus Christ.

Furthermore, increased interest in the historic formularies of the Church of England has been generated by the current painful divisions within the Anglican Communion which inevitably highlight the matter of Anglican identity. In the end our Anglican Foundations cannot be avoided since our identity as Anglicans is intimately related to the question of Christian identity, and Christian identity cannot avoid questions of Christian understanding and belief. While the 39 Articles often become the focus of discussions about Christian and Anglican belief (and have been addressed in this series through *The Faith We Confess* by Gerald Bray) the fact that the 1662 *Book of Common Prayer* and the Ordinal are also part of the doctrinal foundations of the Church of England is often neglected.

Thus the aim of this series of booklets which focus on the Formularies of the Church of England and the elements of the different services within the Prayer Book is to highlight what those services teach about the Christian faith and to demonstrate how they are also designed to shape the practice of that faith. As well as providing an account of the origins of the Prayer Book services, these booklets are designed to offer practical guidance on how such services may be used in Christian ministry nowadays.

It is not necessary to use the exact 1662 services in order to be true to our Anglican heritage, identity and formularies. However if we grasp the principles of Cranmer which underpinned those services then modern versions of them can fulfil the same task of teaching congregations how to live as Christians which Cranmer intended. If we are ignorant of the principles of Cranmer then our Sunday gatherings will inevitably teach something to Anglican congregations, but it will not be the robust biblical faith which Cranmer promoted.

So our hope is that through this Anglican Foundations series our identity as Anglicans will be clarified and that there will be by God's grace a renewal of the teaching and practice of the Christian faith through the services of the Church of England and elsewhere within the Anglican Communion.


Mark Burkill and Gerald Bray

Series Editors, The Latimer Trust

## CONTENTS

*To Caroline,*
*whom God has joined together with me for the past 25 years!*

*Thanks particularly to Revd Dr Andrew Atherstone and Dr Martin Davie for their helpful and incisive comments on this manuscript.*

# 1    Introduction

This Latimer Study will examine the text of the 1662 *Book of Common Prayer* Marriage Service and compare it with biblical teaching on the subject of Marriage, considering the implications of a modern celebration of marriage in today's society. We hope to demonstrate the abiding benefit of this service whilst asking some questions surrounding contemporary challenges to this ancient rite.

## 1.1    *The abiding relevance of Book of Common Prayer "The Solemnization of Matrimony"*

The *Book of Common Prayer* Marriage Service contains some of the most beautiful 16th century prose: "wilt thou have this woman/man to be thy wedded wife/husband, to live together after God's ordinance in the holy estate of Matrimony?"... "for better for worse, for richer for poorer, in sickness and in health, to love, cherish and to obey, till death us do part."..."N. and N. have consented together in holy wedlock, and have witnessed the same before God and this company, and thereto have given and pledged their troth either to the other, and have declared the same by the giving and receiving of a Ring, and by joining of hands; I pronounce that they be Man and Wife together, In the Name of the Father, and of the Son, and of the Holy Ghost. Amen." There is depth and yet a simple profundity here.

But it is not for merely nostalgic reasons that the Church of England continues to cherish the *BCP* marriage service. Here we find, encapsulated in rich language, the reformed theology of Christian marriage, shaped by the Bible.

The Reformers wrestled with the issue of indissolubility, with matters related to the social and familial goods of marriage, all of which are pertinent matters for discussions about marriage today. It is worth noting in passing the wording of this service: it is called "the solemnization of matrimony". The title implies that the role of the clergy is to "solemnise" – that is, to formalise and celebrate – something which is in practice is performed by God. It is God who joins the couple together; the job of the ministry is to prepare the couple for marriage, teach them about God's design for marriage, and then publicly to attest and hear the mutual vows made in the presence of God. More on this as we continue our thoughts on this topic.

There is something here to aid the contemporary controversies surrounding divorce and remarriage, single parenting, civil partnerships and now, same sex marriage. Whilst these issues will not be the primary focus of our discussion, we shall draw out some implications for today from the *BCP* understanding of Marriage along the way.

We shall divide the booklet into the following sections. First, we look at some of the contemporary challenges which provide a backdrop for our discussion. Secondly, we turn to an overview of the biblical teaching on marriage. Next, we will briefly consider the historical context in which the *BCP* marriage service had its genesis. This will lead to a commentary on the text of the *BCP* marriage liturgy. Following this we shall examine a few of the later liturgical developments and observe similarities or dissimilarities which they espouse concerning the doctrine of marriage. Finally, we consider the trajectory in which the marriage service points and how it might provide further direction for ongoing discussions about marriage.

## 2   Contemporary challenges surrounding the nature and purpose of marriage

This booklet is written at a time when the nature and purpose of marriage is under considerable debate.

In 2004 the Government passed a bill approving Civil Partnerships. In 2013 the Same Sex Marriage Bill was passed with the first Same-Sex Marriages taking place on 29th March 2014. The tax privileges previously afforded to heterosexual married couples have in recent years been applied equally to other forms of partnerships. The societal expectations are that same sex marriage should be afforded equal rights and privileges.

These societal expectations are in sharp contrast with the assumptions which underlie the *BCP* Marriage service and all subsequent revisions to the service thus far. The framers of our liturgy are clear that marriage is a public ceremony between two consenting adults of opposite gender, to the exclusion of others, with an expectation of children (if still of childbearing age), and until death dissolves the marriage. The history of the development of the *BCP* liturgy has followed a transition from marriage as a civic function, performed partly in the home but followed by a Church service, to one which is entirely located in the church. We will note that the interplay between the social/cultural and the religious/liturgical function of the marriage service has been a key part of the development of the liturgy down the centuries. We should be aware of the way in which societal expectations of marriage have impacting the shaping of liturgy in the 16th, 17th and 20th Centuries.

Whilst the Church of England has continued to privilege traditional marriage it would be fair to say that at the time of writing there is diminishing general assent to the doctrine of marriage as set out in the introduction to the Book of Common Prayer. The dispute not only relates to whether it is solely one man and one women who are able to be joined together in matrimony; but also the place of child-rearing, the status of "fornication", cohabitation and more informal couplings are up for discussion. We will return to all of these issues.

Of course, those in favour of Same Sex Marriage argue that the Church has changed its stance on marriage over the years as a result of both listening to societal challenges and rereading biblical texts. For example, the Church of England did not officially permit remarriage after divorce until 2002. Even then it seemingly did so rather reluctantly: its canons and doctrine still refer to life-long union. Thus some would argue that the Church of England has been slow to "catch up" with the changes in definition of marriage during its history and we should recognise this in the current discussion about The Marriage (Same Sex Couples) Act 2013. In their response to the change in the legal definition of marriage the House of Bishops issued a Pastoral Letter which concedes that "Same sex relationships often embody genuine mutuality and fidelity, virtues which the Book of Common Prayer uses to commend marriage", whilst at the same time affirming the "Christian understanding and doctrine of marriage as a lifelong union between one man and one women remains unchanged."[1] The Bishops' response may be read as consistent with Canon B30 "Of Holy Matrimony" of the Church of England which states:

1.  The Church of England affirms, according to our Lord's teaching, that marriage is in its nature a union permanent and lifelong, for better for worse, till death them do part, of one man with one woman, to the exclusion of all others on either side, for the procreation and nurture of children, for the hallowing and right direction of the natural instincts and affections, and for the mutual society, help and comfort which the one ought to have of the other, both in prosperity and adversity.

2.  The teaching of our Lord affirmed by the Church of England is expressed and maintained in the Form of Solemnization of Matrimony contained in *The Book of Common Prayer*.

3.  It shall be the duty of the minister, when application is made to him for matrimony to be solemnized in the church of which he is the minister, to explain to the two persons who desire to be married the Church's doctrine of marriage as herein set forth,

---

[1] The text of the Bishops' 2013 Pastoral Letter may be found here: http://www.churchofengland.org/media-centre/news/2014/02/house-of-bishops-pastoral-guidance-on-same-sex-marriage.aspx (accessed 10th March 2014).

and the need of God's grace in order that they may discharge aright their obligations as married persons.[2]

The necessity of the 2013 Bishops' Statement underlines the considerable discussion about the nature and purpose of marriage: in part this has been in response to the societal discussion about Same Sex Marriage, but many other issues have also come into play. For example, the advent of safe and reliable contraception has increasingly enabled a separation of sexual activity from procreation. Women have much more ability to choose if, when and how many, children they may have. Alongside this is the widespread practice (and general acceptance) of cohabitation. Clergy find themselves marrying couples who almost invariably have "lived together" for a time with the marriage service acting as a public declaration and – often expensive – rite of passage. We shall need to grapple with the question: are the cultural and societal changes since 1662 so great that the liturgy which celebrates Marriage in the *Book of Common Prayer* is no longer relevant for today?

Despite these, and many other recent changes, marriage continues to be popular. In 2011 (latest available statistics) just under 250,000 marriages took place in England and Wales. However, 70% of these

---

[2]   The official position of the Church of England on Homosexuality remains the Private Members Motion of November 1987 General Synod, the so-called "Higton Motion", which may be seen to be in line with Canon B30, namely: 'That this Synod affirms that the biblical and traditional teaching on chastity and fidelity in personal relationships in a response to, and expression of, God's love for each one of us, and in particular affirms:
1) that sexual intercourse is an act of total commitment which belongs properly within a permanent married relationship; 2) that fornication and adultery are sins against this ideal, and are to be met by a call to repentance and the exercise of compassion; 3) that homosexual genital acts also fall short of this ideal, and are likewise to be met by a call to repentance and the exercise of compassion; 4) that all Christians are called to be exemplary in all spheres of morality, including sexual morality; and that holiness of life is particularly required of Christian leaders.'
This position is backed up the Report *Issues in Human Sexuality* (1991) and *Some Issues in Human Sexuality* (2003), although the publication of the *Pilling Report* (2013) includes in its recommendations 'This should continue to involve profound reflection on the interpretation and application of Scripture. These conversations should set the discussion of sexuality within the wider context of human flourishing". This "reflection" also includes a fresh examination of the theology of marriage.   https://www.churchofengland.org/our-views/marriage,-family-and-sexuality-issues/human-sexuality/homosexuality.aspx

marriages were civil ceremonies, not religious ceremonies (Anglican or otherwise).[3]

Let us now turn to some of the key biblical texts which undergird *The Book of Common Prayer* understanding of marriage.

---

[3] See data at http://www.ons.gov.uk/ons/rel/vsob1/marriages-in-england-and-wales--provisional-/2011/stb-marriages-in-england-and-wales--provisional---2011.html. This article plots the trends in marriage in England and Wales since 1966 http://www.ons.gov.uk/ons/rel/vsob1/marriages-in-england-and-wales--provisional-/2011/sty-marriages.html

## 3   The Biblical foundation of marriage

The key foundational biblical text is Genesis 2:24: *For this reason a man will leave his father and his mother and be united to his wife, and they will become one flesh.* This text should be read alongside Genesis 1:26-28 which explains the joint function of the couple as they image God through filling the earth with more human beings who will reveal the rule of the King over his creation.

Derek Kidner explains the drama of Genesis 2:23f:

> The naming of the animals, a scene which portrays man as a monarch of all he surveys, poignantly reveals him as a social being, made for fellowship, not power: he will not live until he loves, giving himself away (v.24) to another on his own level. So the woman is presented wholly as his partner and counterpart; nothing is yet said of her as a child bearer. She is valued for herself alone.[1]

Clearly, the author of Genesis believes her role as a child-bearer is important, but this significance is not named as part of the original creation. The emphasis is first placed upon their union together as one flesh.

The context of the creation of the woman is that *no suitable helper is found for Adam* amongst the animal kingdom (Genesis 2:20b). There has been considerable discussion over whether woman is created to meet the man's loneliness, or whether the creation of the woman was in order to help Adam better fulfil the creation mandate (to rule over creation and fill the world with God's image bearers, see Genesis 1:26-28).[2] Alongside the Genesis 2 context we will also need to consider the subsequent use of Genesis 2:24 in the New Testament in order to answer the question about the purpose of marriage.

### 3.1   *Created as one flesh*

First, note the special attention given to the creation of the woman. Adam is put into a deep sleep and God removes one of his ribs to form the

---

[1]   Derek Kidner, *Genesis* (Cambridge: Tyndale Press, 1967), p 65.
[2]   Christopher Ash addresses this issue in "The Purpose of Marriage", *Churchman* Vol 115, No 1, pp 17-29.

woman (2:21-22). Originally they were one flesh for she is made from the one man. She is made from Adam's rib, not from the dust of the earth.

## 3.2   Complementing each other

Secondly, the man is delighted with the woman, now displayed by God before his eyes. He poetically exclaims: *"this is now bone of my bones and flesh of my flesh; she shall be called 'woman' for she was taken out of man."* (2:23). Matthew Henry's oft quoted comment captures this well:

> The woman was made of a rib out of the side of Adam; not made out of his head to rule over him, nor out of his feet to be trampled upon by him, but out of his side to be equal with him, under his arm to be protected, and near his heart to be beloved.[3]

Even before we read the words of v.24 we hear from Adam's lips words of satisfaction and delight. There is something in the creation of Eve that meets his loneliness, which, in a sense makes him complete. She is to be, literally "a helper as opposite him" (or "corresponding to him").[4]

## 3.3   Uniting with each other

Thirdly, the threefold process of marriage (Genesis 2:24) is explained as: "Leave"; "Cleave"; "Become one flesh". "God himself, like a father of the bride, leads the woman to the man".[5] In their perfect state ("naked; with no shame") the union is set.

> The removal of the piece of the man in order to create the woman implies that from now on neither is complete without the other. The man needs the woman for his wholeness, and the woman needs the man for hers.[6]

This is no mere social convenience, nor is it merely a religious custom. They are reunited at the deepest level of creation, bringing them back into the union, that in one sense they previously knew.

The act of marriage is then summarised as follows:

---

[3]   Matthew Henry, *A Commentary on the Whole Bible.* Vol 1 *Genesis – Deuteronomy,* (Word publishing, no date).

[4]   Kidner, *Genesis,* p 65.

[5]   G. Von Rad, *Genesis: A Commentary* (London: SCM, 1972), p 82.

[6]   D. Atkinson, *The Message of Genesis 1-11* (Nottingham: IVP, 1990), p 71.

### 3.3.1 A man will leave his father and mother...

They leave their respective family units and set up a new household together. Their new loyalty to each other is even higher than to their parental obligations;

### 3.3.2 {he will} be united to his wife ...

Their new union is societal (in the sense that they form a new community) and physical (in the sense that the sexual relationship helps "join them together"). Israel was told to cleave to the Lord (Deuteronomy 10:20; 11:22; 13:5) by forsaking all other gods. It may be that there are hints of a covenant understanding here.[7]

### 3.3.3 They will become one flesh...

the married couple are treated, no longer as single image bearers of God (Genesis 1:27) but also, in some respects as "one flesh", that is, one body, and thus one single unit. Lewes Smedes puts it well:

> Sexual intercourse is thus given a meaning: it is meant to express, consolidate and deepen the "one flesh" union of man and wife, as they grow more and more together in a relationship which expresses something of God.[8]

They become one flesh through their intentional union, but this becomes more and more a reality as they unite sexually and procreatively.

> By leaving of father and mother, which applies to the woman as well as to the man, the conjugal union is shown to be a spiritual oneness, a vital communion of heart as well as of body, in which it finds its consummation. This union is of a totally different nature from that of parents and children; hence marriage between parents and children is entirely opposed to the ordinance of God.[9]

### 3.3.4 They knew no shame (v.25).

Von Rad points out that shame is a puzzling human phenomenon, but that this verse "speaks of it as a phenomenon that is inseparable from

---

[7] See G. J. Wenham, *Genesis 1-49* Word Biblical Commentary vol 1 (Dallas, Texas: Word Books, 1991), p 71.

[8] Lewis Smedes, *Sex in the Real World* (Tring, Herts: Lion, 1979), p 14.

[9] Von Rad, *Genesis: A Commentary*, pp 90f.

sexuality".[10] In their state of innocence they enjoyed contentedness and unhindered intimacy in the one-flesh relationship.

The implications of Genesis 2 are huge for our discussion about the Marriage Service and the subsequent expression of marriage in modern society. It touches on issues concerning the "indissolubility" of marriage, of the social "good" of marriage, and it addresses questions about same sex marriage and the role of the household.

## 3.4   *Intended for each other*

Fourthly, Genesis 2:24 is also a key text for answering the question: "why did God make marriage?" We look at the three places where this verse is cited in the New Testament.

This verse is quoted by Jesus as evidence for the God-intended foundational understanding of marriage and thus the reason why divorce is never his ideal. Jesus says that Moses allowed for divorce because the people's hearts were hardened (see Matthew 19:4-6). This would seem to provide some support for the discussion about permanency and indissolubility which may be inferred in the BCP marriage service.

Genesis 2:24 is also quoted in 1 Corinthians 6:16 in a context where Paul warns that the Corinthian church's perception that "what you do with your body does not matter" (whether that be eating food or sexual intercourse, the Corinthians did not have a Christian understanding of the body, vv12ff). Christians are united with Christ and thereby they become one body/flesh with him. Thus to join in sexual relations with a prostitute is to use "one flesh" language (in the physical function of sex) with no intention of truly becoming "one flesh" at a social/communal level with the other person. The Corinthians should *flee from sexual immorality* (v.18). None of the three reasons the BCP gives for marriage (children, remedy against sin, mutual help and comfort) are met through fleeting sexual encounters.

Next we note that the quotation of Genesis 2:24 in Ephesians 5:31 is particularly significant in appreciating the purpose of marriage. The submission of the wife to the husband, and the requirement of the husband to love his wife sacrificially, is an important backdrop to the

---

[10]   Von Rad, *Genesis: A Commentary*, p 85.

introductory section of the marriage service and the exchanging of the vows.

Moreover, the influence of Ephesians 5 on the framing of the liturgy and theology of the *BCP* Marriage service is clear in the following ways:

### 3.4.1    Mystery

Having quoted Genesis 2:24 Paul then goes on to say: *This is a profound mystery – but I am talking about Christ and the Church.* (Ephesians 5:32). In the BCP Marriage Service Cranmer departed from the Medieval view of marriage as a sacrament. The theological contention in Ephesians 5 relates to the nature of the "mystery", understood by the Catholic church to refer to a sacrament, but by Cranmer to refer to something else.

The word *mysterion* also occurs in Ephesians 1:9; 3:4ff and 6:19. In each of these uses the word takes on a similar meaning, not referring to a sacrament, but rather God's fuller unveiling of something which was previously hidden.[11] Paul assumes that those living after Jesus' first coming are privileged with a greater appreciation and a sense of consummation, now seen in the full revelation of the Gospel in Jesus Christ. In Ephesians 3 Paul explains that the inclusion of the Gentiles in God's saving purposes, making them heirs together with Israel, is making plain that which was not previously fully appreciated by former generations. This implies that marriage, as conceived in Ephesians 5, is intended to support God's mission to the world. Marriage signifies the "mystical union that is between Christ and the Church". More on this in a moment.

### 3.4.2    Mutuality

In a similar way, Paul explains that marriage is to be viewed as a complementary union of husband and wife: the wife submitting to her husband as the Church submits to Christ, and the husband loving the wife as Christ loved the Church. This may now been seen to demonstrate how marriage is intended by God to be a living, breathing illustration of Christ's relationship with his Bride, the Church.

---

[11]    Since the 1215 Fourth Lateran Council (and subsequently confirmed at the Councils of Lyon II (1247), Florence (1439) and Trent (1547)) the Catholic Church has recognised seven sacraments: baptism, confirmation, the Eucharist, penance, anointing of the sick, ordination, and matrimony as the places where God imparts grace to his people. Protestants only believe Holy Communion and Baptism to be sacraments.

In Ephesians, Paul assumes that the complementarity of the man and the woman is something to be celebrated and, moreover, is inextricably tied up with Christ's relationship with the Church.

First, verse 22 indicates that the wife should see beyond the loving lead of the husband to the Lord (see v.25). *hupotasso* (generally translated as "submit") implies a voluntary deference out of love. The wife's submission to the husband is of the same sort as her submission to the Lord.

Secondly, husbands are to love their wives as Christ loved the Church (v.25). Christ's love of the Church is described in the aorist tense: it is demonstrated in the past, in a supreme act of self-giving, climaxing on the cross. Such love is costly, self-sacrificial and the model for husband-love.

The key thing here is that both husband and wife are called to total self-surrender to the other, not looking to their own rights, but rather to that of their spouse. For the wife, she demonstrates this in her submission. For the husband, this is demonstrated in his sacrificial love.

Those who consider men and women to be made equal by God but complementary in the roles which they fulfil in the family and the Church are usually referred to as complementarians. They point out that the complementary mutuality (in the form of headship and submission) is not a result of the Fall, but rather is to be found in the God given created differences between male and female.[12] However, it is twisted and marred by the Fall. Instead of a loving lead the husband is inclined to domineer (Genesis 3:16b.). The wife is viewed as allowing herself to be deceived and heeding the serpent's lies rather than the instruction of God. Both parties blame the other for their failure (Genesis 3:1-6, 12).

The *BCP* liturgy implies that as the couple live out their marriage according to the promises made one to another in the marriage liturgy, they will thereby demonstrate their love. In marriage, they are "one flesh" and both the wife and the husband are intended to complement each other by their respective submission and love; "after all, no one ever hated his own body...." (Ephesians 5:29). The day by day, week by

---

[12] See Latimer publication by Ben Cooper, *Positive Complementarianism* (London: Latimer Trust, 2014), for a summary of these arguments.

week, year by year, decade by decade of loving and submitting one to another is the best means whereby they both give and receive love. This point is developed further in the Homily "Of the State of Matrimony" (see below).

### 3.4.3 Mission

For these reasons, then, marriage is not purely a private affair, or merely a satisfaction of the desire for intimacy or just a remedy against loneliness. Neither is marriage purely about the functionality of the husband and the wife sharing together in ruling the world and filling it with image bearers (cf Genesis 1:26.-28). Whilst both intimacy and functionality are clearly implied in Genesis 2, and also in the *BCP* Marriage Service, the ultimate goal of marriage is to be seen as demonstrating God's soteriological and eschatological purposes through the Church. Marriage, according to Ephesians 5:21ff, acts as a testimony to the world of God's saving action. This ultimate purpose of marriage will also be found in the *BCP* service too.[13] The principle *lex orandi, lex credendi* ("the law of praying is the law of belief") applies to the Marriage Service as to all of the Church of England liturgies. In other words, we find the doctrine of the Church of England best expressed in its liturgies.[14]

The mission focus of marriage is to be understood in the way in which the "mystery" unfolds God's fuller saving plans. Peter O'Brien points out that marriage is to be understood typologically, as revealing God's relationship with his people:

> The first Adam's love for his wife as *one flesh* with himself and the last Adam's love for his own bride, his body, are... the typology [that] serves Paul's pastoral purpose of providing a model for Christian marriage which is grounded in primeval human origins and reflective of ultimate divine reality.[15]

Christ centred marriages and mutually deferential marriages (the wife submitting; the husband loving) eagerly anticipate the eschatological

---

[13] We will explore each of these ideas as they occur in the text of The Marriage Service, but the reader might also like to consult Simon Vibert *The Diamond Marriage* (Fearn, Scotland: Christian Focus: 1997) for more detail on this subject.
[14] W. Taylor Stevenson's helpful chapter on this subject may be found in eds. Stephen Sykes & John Booty, *The Study of Anglicanism* (London: SPCK, 1988, 1995), Part IV, Ch 6, pp 174-187.
[15] P.T. O'Brien, *The Letter to the Ephesians* (Nottingham: Apollos, 1999), quoting R.C. Ortland, pp 432f.

fulfilment of God's purposes. In that day there will be no more marrying or giving in marriage (Matthew 22:30). And in anticipation of that day, human marriage looks forward to the marriage feast of the Lamb (Matthew 19:6-9).

Kasper puts it well:

> Marriage is a sign of eschatological hope. The festive mood at a wedding is a symbol of the joy and the fulfilment of human hopes that will be present at the end of time (see Mark 2:19ff., Matthew 2:1-11, 25:1-13 etc.). It is therefore not simply necessary from the human point of view alone to celebrate the wedding as festively as possible, it is important to mark the occasion in this way as a hopeful anticipation and celebration in advance of the feast at the end of time.[16]

In this respect, human marriage is penultimate, not ultimate. The ultimate goal is the unity of the Lord with his bride, the perfect and spotless church.

God has ordained marriage to be a visual aid for the world of the kind of intimacy for which he is preparing his people at the end time celebration. In other words, it would seem, marriage has been created by God so that through the dynamics of love and submission in marriage the world will be able to see how Christ loved the church sacrificially, and how the church is to respond in submission to Him. Consequently, not only does marriage have a clear eschatological focus, but every marriage, to a greater or lesser extent, embodies an evangelistic message for the watching world. God will indeed bring all things to unity under Christ the head. Such marriages are God's powerful visual aid of his soteriological purposes, "signifying unto us the mystical union that is betwixt Christ and his Church..."[17]

See Excursus (page 52 below) for a brief discussion on the implications of Genesis 2:24 and the issue of Divorce and Remarriage.

Having spent some time on the foundational biblical texts we now turn to the *BCP* Marriage Service.

---

[16]  W. Kasper, *Theology of Christian Marriage* (London: Burns & Oates, 1980), pp 42-43.
[17]  I draw out the implications of this thesis in more detail in *The Diamond Marriage*.

# 4  History of the Prayer Book Marriage service

We begin our study of the elegant language of the text of the *BCP* Marriage Service in the world of the 16th and 17th century and then we consider later revisions of this service (particularly the *Alternative Service Book*, 1980, and the *Common Worship* services, 2000). We shall conclude by examining some of the challenges which the *BCP* marriage service presents for a modern understanding of marriage. We have in mind a number of questions: Undoubtedly beautiful, but is the language of the *BCP* still relevant? Moreover, the greater question is: what is the theology of this service and how reflective is it of the biblical understanding of marriage? Thus, how might the *BCP* marriage service resonate with a contemporary understanding of marriage, and is it still fit for purpose for today's weddings?

## 4.1  *The gradual departure from the Sarum rite*

It is important to appreciate the process of arriving at the text of the 1662 *Book of Common Prayer*. The first two editions (1549 and 1552) mark a transition from the modest revisions of the Medieval liturgies (in 1549) to a more substantive Protestant theology (in 1552). This is seen most obviously in the Holy Communion Service, but the changes to the marriage service are also to be viewed through the lens of a reformed view of the role of the sacraments.[1]

The brilliant work of Archbishop Thomas Cranmer (1489-1555) gave liturgical shape to the large theological shifts that marked the departure from Medieval theology to Protestant theology.

The 1662 *Book of Common Prayer* is still the official liturgy of the Church of England.[2] The 1662 *BCP* is substantially based upon the Edward VI[th] 1552 liturgies, although with some "concessions", e.g. the reintroduction of the "manual acts" in the Holy Communion liturgy.

---

[1]  See Marion Hatchett in Eds. Stephen Sykes & John Booty, *The Study of Anglicanism* (London: SPCK, 1988, 1995), Part IV, Ch 1, and also Nigel Scotland, *The Supper: Cranmer and Communion* (London: Latimer Trust, 2013), pp.6-9.

[2]  Of course, most Church of England Churches do not use the *BCP* as their main service book, thus the question must be asked "to what extent do we now have a "common" prayer book?" We will return to this matter shortly.

The most significant changes to the theology of the Church of England might be observed in the liturgies for Baptism and the Lord's Supper (the two sacraments recognised by the Protestant Church). The single biggest change to the marriage service is the rejection of marriage as a sacrament and inculcation of a more Protestant view of marriage. Subtle changes to the marriage service mark this change in understanding.

According to the Council of Trent (1545-1563), marriage between two baptised people is to be considered a sacrament:

> If any one shall say that matrimony is not truly and properly one of the Seven Sacraments of the Evangelical Law, instituted by Christ our Lord, but was invented in the Church by men, and does not confer grace, let him be anathema.[3]

This understanding of marriage was denied by Martin Luther, who was of course to marry the nun Katherine von Bora in the summer of 1525. Luther famously confessed to his friend Wenceslaus Link "the Lord has plunged me into marriage", which made the angels laugh and the devils weep![4] Similarly, in a typically robust manner, John Calvin spoke of the new found joy in the holy ordinance of marriage:

> The last one is marriage. All men admit that it was instituted by God (Genesis 2:21-24; Matthew 19:4ff.); but no man ever saw it administered as a sacrament until the time of Gregory. And what sober man would ever have thought it such? Marriage is a good and holy ordinance of God; and farming, building, cobbling and barbering are lawful ordinances of God, and yet are not sacraments. For it is required that a sacrament be not only a work of God but an outward ceremony appointed by God to confirm a promise. Even children can discern that there is no such thing in matrimony.[5]

The rejection of a sacramental understanding of marriage is evident in Cranmer's revisions to the Sarum marriage rite. There are several examples of this: first, the focus is very much upon the mutuality of promises made between husband and wife, not on the role of the priest

[3] Canon 10, Session 24, Council of Trent 1563, see Norman Tanner (Ed), *Decrees of the Ecumenical Councils*, Vol 2, (London: Sheed & Ward, 1990), p 744.

[4] Philip Schaff, *History of the Christian Church*, Volume VII. *Modern Christianity. The German Reformation.*

[5] John Calvin, (Ed. J. T. McNeill, Tr F.L. Battles), *The Institutes of The Christian Religion*, IV, xix, (Philadelphia: The Wesminter Press, 1960), pp 1480f. first published in Latin in 1536 with the French translation following in 1541.

in securing their mystical union; secondly, in the giving and receiving of rings, these are "tokens" of the couple's love; they are not blessed by the Priest; the Priest does not preside over a sacrament but rather pronounces God's promise and blessing. There are no candles, blessed water and repeated blessings. Moreover, the priest witnesses the exchange of vows and presides over the ceremony but it is quite clear that it is God alone who can do the "joining" of them together.[6] There are other changes which will which we will consider along the way, but many of these are subtle and do not mark a large departure from the shape of the Sarum rite.[7]

The main changes in Cranmer's rite could are best summarised as "reformed theology" in "post-medieval dress" as Kenneth Stevenson notes:

> There is both continuity and discontinuity [with the Sarum rite]. For those who wanted no marriage service at all, or a bare one, it is called "*solemnization* of matrimony", and yet it is not defined as a sacrament. For those who want to keep the ring, it is still there, but now placed in the *left* hand...and it is placed "on the book" before being given, though it is not blessed.[8]

Along with the rest of the *BCP* liturgy, Cranmer's aim is to make it less ritualistic and less focussed on the Priest:

> This is consistent with the changes already made to the *BCP* Holy Communion service: Since in the late medieval period Eucharistic piety had come to centre on the elevation of the elements at the Institution Narrative, and Cranmer wished to recover a Eucharistic piety centred on the receiving of the sacrament, the elevations which had been introduced at that point in the late thirteenth and fourteenth centuries were forbidden – the only ceremonial actions to be explicitly prohibited.[9]

The marriage service too, now no longer a sacrament, is also to be less "complicated"; ritual is kept to the minimum. The priest is witness to a public ceremony but nothing mystical is happening (in the sacramental sense), rather, here is an opportunity for teaching about marriage and

---

[6]   Kenneth Stevenson, *Nuptial Blessings* (London: SPCK, 1982), p 140.
[7]   Stevenson, *Nuptial Blessings* is helpful on this point, see pp 134-152.
[8]   Stevenson, *Nuptial Blessings,* p 139.
[9]   Marion Hatchett in Eds. Stephen Sykes & John Booty, *The Study of Anglicanism* (London: SPCK, 1988, 1995), Part IV, Ch 1, p 128.

public prayer for the couple and intercession for God to join the couple together in holy matrimony. However, whilst rejecting marriage as a sacrament, Cranmer did not see it as a purely secular affair. It is a means of grace through which they may receive God's blessing. It was also expected that the newly married couple would take the sacrament of Holy Communion, underlying the essentially Christian nature of the service. Finally, as we shall explore further below, in Cranmer's mind marriage fulfils the mandate to procreate and fill the earth with further images of God, thus fulfilling the Abrahamic promise (Genesis 12:2-3), thus children will be "brought up in the fear and nurture of the Lord, and to the praise of his holy Name".

## 4.2 *The new cultural expression encompassed in the Prayer Book revisions*

The changes made to the liturgical shape of the *Book of Common Prayer* also reveal quite a lot about the societal and cultural views of marriage taking place in during this period. Bruce W Young, writing about the role of religion and family life during the Shakespearean era (1564-1616), has made the following observation:

> The age of Shakespeare was a time of transition during which the traditional outlook continued, even dominated, and yet was also challenged. The challenges came in various forms, including the beginnings of modern science and philosophy and movement toward greater religious and political freedom and pluralism. Such changes eventually led to the decline of the traditional outlook and to a split between the public sphere (where a more secular outlook prevailed) and the private sphere (the sphere of religious belief and personal relationships).[10]

Shakespeare's writings reflected the dominant view that the household is a safe unit of mutuality and trust, with permeable outside edges (to include servants and extended family). Its central role in society is undisputed.

Whilst there has been much written about the formal marriage arrangements of wealthy and aristocratic weddings, less is known about 16th and 17th century marriage practices in the less well-to-do households.

---

[10]  Bruce W. Young, *Family Life in the Age of Shakespeare* (London: Greenwood Press, 2009), p 28.

Alan Macfarlane refers to research which suggests that the average age of the groom was between 25 and 30, and the bride between 20 and 30. Payments of dowries and future living arrangements were a matter of discussion, influenced by the relative wealth/property ownership of the two parties. He cites evidence that "romantic love" was increasingly given as a reason for marriage and that parental consent was not always sought (something which is reflected in several of Shakespeare's plays). Within the church, proposal, the publication of Banns and a form of "courtship" meant that it was likely to be at least six months between betrothal and marriage itself.[11]

Macfarlane also points to the role of the household during this time period. Sometimes the post wedding celebrations were divided into two parts, one at the bride's father's house and another at the groom's house. Others (such as Patrick Collinson) have argued that the Reformation itself precipitated the full impact of societal changes which took place in 16th and 17th century England, including in marriage.[12] The impact on Priests alone was huge, not least with the champion of the Continental Reformation, Martin Luther, marrying Katherine von Bora in Germany. It was now marriage and childrearing that was thought to be the norm for the priestly household, rather than the celibate life. This brought a breath of fresh air blowing through the church's attitude to sex, childbirth, work, and a more integrated outlook on life.

In 16th and 17th century England, the household provided the basic building blocks of society. Society was defined, not by individuals, but by households: these were not private secluded homes (of the kind we know in the 21st Century), but often housed extended families including wives, children, siblings, aunts/uncles, servants etc. Life was lived in the presence – and often full visibility – of others in the community. Moreover, for the Protestant family, the household was the place where the father took over the role of spiritual mentor, ensuring that the household worshipped as well as worked together.

---

[11] Alan Macfarlane "The Informal Social Control of Marriage in Seventeenth Century England; Some Preliminary Notes", in Fox, Vivian & Quitt, Martin, *Loving, Parenting and Dying. The Family Cycle in England and America, Past and Present* (New York: Psychohistory Press, 1980), pp 110-111.

[12] "The Protestant Family" in *The Birthpangs of Protestant England, Religious and Cultural change in the Sixteenth and Seventeenth Centuries*, (Basingstoke: Macmillan, 1988.), pp 60-93.

There is some evidence that a part of the Catholic marriage service took place in the home before moving to a celebration of the Mass in Church. We have already noted in his introduction to the 1549 Prayer Book Cranmer is particularly critical of fussiness and incomprehensibility. His liturgy was designed to be accessible to the whole household, and intelligible to all. So the movement of the *BCP* liturgy is from the entrance to the church building to the gathered congregation (with Holy Communion as an option). It is a public ceremony before the family and local community. The liturgical revisions themselves were consonant with the biblical appreciation of the continuity and mutuality between the home (the Household) and the Church (the Household of God). For Cranmer, the household of God and the household of the Church were the two key foundations of society. Hence, the Presbyter is to manage his family and household well because failure to do so disqualifies him from managing the household of God (see 1 Timothy 3:4f.). The responsibility of parenthood and pastor-hood are equally demanding.[13]

## 4.3 The 17th century revival of healthy marriage

J.I. Packer has noted that the Puritans built on the Protestant revival of a much more healthy and biblical view of sex and intimacy in marriage. Like Luther and Calvin, Cranmer should be seen as part of a new movement which unravelled some distorted views of sex and marriage:

> Chrysostom had denied that Adam and Eve could have had sexual relations before the Fall; Augustine allowed that procreation was lawful, but insisted that the passions accompanying intercourse were always sinful... Gregory of Nyssa was sure that Adam and Eve had been made without sexual desire, and that had there been no Fall mankind would have produced by means of what Leland Ryken gravely calls "some harmless mode of vegetation"... so twisted a record urgently needed to be set straight, and this the Reformers, followed by the Puritans, forthrightly did.[14]

---

[13] See Jim Hurley *Man and Woman in Biblical Perspective*, (Eugene, Origen: Wipf & Stock Publishers, 2002) for more on this theme.

[14] J.I. Packer, *Among God's Giants* (Eastbourne: Kingsway, 1991), p 343.

The *BCP* marriage service reflects a view of marriage which was consistent with the divinely given parabolic nature of marriage. For example, on the other side of the Atlantic, Jonathan Edwards:[15]

> The mutual joy of Christ and his church is like that of bridegroom and bride, in that they rejoice in each other as those whom they have chosen above others, for their nearest, most intimate, and everlasting friends and companions...

> Christ and his church, like the bridegroom and the bride, rejoice in each other, as those that are the objects of each other's most tender and ardent love. The love of Christ to his church is altogether unparalleled: the height and depth and length and breadth of it pass knowledge: for he loved the church and gave himself for it; and his love to her proved stronger than death. And on the other hand, she loves him with all her heart. Her whole soul is offered up to him in the flame of love.[16]

This 'strong love'[17] and unbridled commitment was evident in his marriage to Sarah, and illustrates why, for the Puritans, marriage was so important.

Secondly, writing in a context much closer to being contiguous with Cranmer, Richard Baxter provides a robust view of the attractiveness of marriage. Admittedly, the Puritan view of pleasure and a pleasurable outlook on life is seriously doubted by many, but J.I. Packer points to the Puritan love of the created world, their delight in friendship and their belief in the ideal of marriage and family. Plus

> The Puritans, like the Reformers, glorified marriage in conscious contradiction of the medieval idea that celibacy as practised by clergy, monks, and nuns is better – more virtuous – more Christ-like, more pleasing to God – than marriage, procreation, and family life.[18]

---

[15] Strictly speaking Jonathan Edwards was not a Puritan (and of course in New, not old, England!). However Packer is surely right to note that "Puritanism is what Edwards was" (Packer, *Among God's Giants*, p 409).

[16] The sermon "The Church's marriage to her sons, and to her God", *The Works of Jonathan Edwards (Vol.2)*, (Edinburgh: Banner of Truth Trust, 1997), pp 17-26.

[17] See my article on Jonathan Edwards' loves http://archive.churchsociety.org/churchman/documents/Cman_117_4_Vibert.pdf

[18] Packer, *Among God's Giants* p 342.

Baxter might be seen to typify such a Puritan view that marriage was for mutual pleasure and enjoyment in the sight of God:

I pray you, tell me my duty to my wife and hers to me.

The common duty of husband and wife is,

I. Entirely to love each other; and therefore chose one that is truly lovely...and avoid all things that tend to quench your love.

II. To dwell together and enjoy each other, and faithfully join as helpers in the education of their children, the government of the family, and the management of the worldly business.

III. Especially to be helpers of each other's salvation: to stir up each other to faith, love and obedience, and good works: to warn and help each other against sin, and all temptations; to join in God's worship in the family, and in private: to prepare each other for the approach of death, and comfort each other in the hopes of life eternal.

IV. To avoid all dissensions, and to bear with those infirmities in each other which you cannot cure: to assuage, and not provoke, unruly passions; and, in lawful things, to please each other.

V. To keep conjugal chastity and fidelity, and to avoid all unseemly and immodest carriage with another, which may stir up jealousy; and yet to avoid all jealousy which is unjust.

VI. To help one another to bear their burdens (and not by impatience to make them greater). In poverty, crosses, sickness, dangers, to comfort and support each other. And to be delightful companions in holy love, and heavenly hopes and duties, when all other outward comforts fail.[19]

Let us now turn to the text of the Marriage Service and explore how some of these themes are developed.

---

[19] Quoted in Packer, *Among God's Giants*, p 409.

## 5    Commentary on the text: "The Solemnization of Matrimony"

The Publication of the Banns precedes the marriage service in continuity with the formalisation of the practice since Canon 51 of the Lateran IV Council in 1215.[1] A wider variety of options for "marriage by license" exists today, not least because modern communities are more dispersed and knowledge of the familial state of those being married is much less certain than it might have been in 16th Century England.

*Dearly beloved, we are gathered together here in the sight of God, and in the face of this congregation,*

The marriage is a public gathering not merely a private/personal affair. Historians are right to point out that various civic and social arrangements were made in the 16th and 17th century to confirm and confer the public status of marriage. Plus, it may be that some of the service previously happened in the home. Thus it may also be true that the Church in the 16th century is adding a more formal dimension to marriage by strengthening the religious side of marriage in a public ceremony. Nevertheless, these opening words of the Marriage service might be seen to resonate best with Genesis 2, as Von Rad suggests, where God acts as Father of the Bride bringing her to unite, in his presence, with her husband.

Thus there are said to be two witnesses to the marriage: God; and the gathered congregation.

*to join together this Man and this Woman in holy Matrimony; which is an honourable estate, instituted of God in the time of man's innocency,*

The joining together is between one man and one woman. Informal unions between one man and many women were not unknown in the 16th Century. But they were never countenanced in law or in Church.[2]

"Join together" hints at the indissoluble nature of matrimony: "The two shall become one flesh". We have noted that the Genesis account

---

[1]    Clandestine marriages and witness to them by a priest are forbidden. Marriages to be contracted must be published in the churches by the priests so that, if legitimate impediments exist, they may be made known. If doubt exists, let the contemplated marriage be forbidden till the matter is cleared up.
http://www.fordham.edu/halsall/basis/lateran4.asp.

[2]    Macfarlane, "The Informal Social Control of Marriage", pp 110-111.

speaks of a joining that is both social and sexual, and one in which God presides over ceremony and He does the joining. Hence Paul, quoting Genesis 2:24 can say: "one who unites with a prostitute is one with her". In other words, there is a form of union which comes through the sexual act, but the more significant union is with the Lord (1 Corinthians 6:15-17). The *BCP* service implies that the union is more than sexual and includes this necessity of a public joining. Once the public ceremony is complete and the marriage is consummated by the newly married couple then the marriage can be said to have taken place.[3]

Some Continental Reformers believed that the State had the right to pronounce divorce for adultery and other grounds, with Luther and Bucer arguing that the state could execute the adulterer, thus freeing the remaining partner to remarry.[4] English Reformers seem less persuaded by this argument. Whilst rejecting the Catholic understanding of *mysterion*, nevertheless Cranmer's liturgy points to the strong bind between husband and wife in marriage and that the marriage can only be dissolved by God (the "joining together" is pronounced later in the service, see below).

In the 16th Century various Bills proposing the legalization of the dissolution of marriage on the grounds of adultery were brought to Parliament but never made it to the statute book.[5]

As with many of the modest changes made in Cranmer's liturgy much of the content of the text shows consistency with the Sarum rite (albeit with "Reformed Dress"): whilst rejecting the sacramental understanding of marriage, nevertheless not going as far as the continental reformers, who wished for a Christianised government to

---

[3]  Catholic Canon 1051 states that a marriage can be dissolved by the Pope if consummation has not happened. "A valid marriage between baptised persons is said to be merely ratified, if it is not consummated; ratified and consummated, if the spouses have in a human manner engaged together in a conjugal act in itself apt for the generation of offspring. To this act marriage is by its nature ordered and by it the spouses become one flesh." This is amplified (but not undone by) The Matrimony Causes Act (1907) see http://www.legislation.gov.uk/ukpga/1973/18c.

[4]  See H. J. Selderhuis, *Marriage and Divorce in the Thought of Martin Bucer* (Kirksville, Missouri: Truman State University Press, 1999), p 65.

[5]  *Putting Asunder. A Divorce Law for Contemporary Society.* The Report of A Group appointed by the Archbishop of Canterbury in January 1964, (London: SPCK, 1966). This report was commissioned to examine changes in the law that allowed divorce on the basis of common consent.

enforce penalties for immorality. Even the modest changes proposed in the 16th Century Bills did not go as far as those proposed by the Continental Reformers.

Marriage is described as "an honourable estate", not least because it is a "creation ordinance", that is, instituted at the original creation (recorded in Genesis 1-2), before the Fall, and deemed to be good both for believer and non-believer. Hence, most clergy would be happy to marry those who are not Christians if they are prepared to make the vows contained in this service. Marriage was introduced during the "time of man's innocency". It was not an afterthought, nor merely a way to restrain humanity's ill-disciplined sexual appetites. Marriage, as defined by God, is "honourable and holy."

> *signifying unto us the mystical union that is betwixt Christ and his Church;*

The "mystical union" spoken of here speaks of the "mystery" (of Ephesians 5:32). We have already noted that Cranmer reflects the Protestant view that marriage is not a sacrament, but rather performs the function of revealing the union between Christ and his Church. The human institution of marriage is designed to reveal the eschatological union between Christ and His Church.

> *which holy estate Christ adorned and beautified with his presence and first miracle that he wrought, in Cana of Galilee; and is commended of Saint Paul to be honourable among all men:*

Christ's presence at the Wedding in Cana where he performed the first miraculous sign (recorded in John 2) indicates his blessing of marriage. He witnessed the celebration and miraculously provided choice wine, saving an awful social faux pas and endorsing the joy of the occasion.

The teaching of the Apostle Paul also commends this holy estate: the most obvious biblical text to which this probably refers is "Marriage is honourable in all, and the bed undefiled: but whoremongers and adulterers God will judge." (Hebrews 13:4), given that in the 16th Century the authorship of Hebrews was generally thought to be Pauline. Nevertheless, Paul's teaching is also consistent with this theology: he writes, "It is God's will that you should be sanctified: that you should avoid sexual immorality; that each of you should learn to control your own body in a way that is holy and honourable...." (1 Thessalonians 4:3f).

*and therefore is not by any to be enterprised, nor taken in hand, unadvisedly, lightly, or wantonly, to satisfy men's carnal lusts and appetites, like brute beasts that have no understanding; but reverently, discreetly, advisedly, soberly, and in the fear of God; duly considering the causes for which Matrimony was ordained.*

Marriage should not be undertaken impulsively; seeking advice from others is wise; Marriage should not be viewed as the way to sate carnal appetites or lust.[6] Human beings have a higher calling than other creatures. Nothing else in all creation can satisfy the man's loneliness or be a suitable helper for him (Genesis 3:18ff.). The words "brute beasts" seem to be taken from 2 Peter 2:12; Jude 1:10, where both verses speak of the unreasoning and slanderous nature of false teachers. It could be argued that alluding to these words in the context of the marriage service does not best fit the context in which they occur in the New Testament.

Marriage should only be undertaken after counsel from others, due consideration, and in the "cold light of day", and with an appreciation that God is the unseen third party in every wedding. Moreover, an appreciation of the purpose of marriage to unfold the "mystery" of Christ and his bride (Ephesians 5:32) should be part of the teaching preparation for every couple, and the due "consideration of causes [i.e. reasons] for which matrimony was ordained".

*First, It was ordained for the procreation of children, to be brought up in the fear and nurture of the Lord, and to the praise of his holy Name.*

The liturgy places "procreation" as the first reason for marriage. For some this is thought to be less relevant since the advent of fairly reliable contraception, enabling couples to choose if, when and how many children they may have (although some recognition needs to be made that some cannot choose to have children for various reasons).[7] Some

---

[6] I have noticed that Christians often marry at a young age because they have heard the message "sexual relationships are for the marriage bed alone". Quite often this has resulted in them marrying younger than they would otherwise have done (because they want sex but know it to be wrong outside of marriage) and this has caused other problems in terms of immaturity, or being sure that the person they are marrying is truly the best life-partner for them. Better teaching of our teenagers and pre-marital counselling will help.

[7] The Roman Catholic Church still teaches that contraception is wrong. Given the modest revisions from the Sarum rite one can envisage how child birth might still be seen to be a primary reason for marriage.

have taken this to mean that marriage should not take place between those who are beyond childbearing age. However, we also noted that Genesis 2:23-24 implies that a marriage is a true marriage even prior to (or possibly even without?) the birth of children.

Interestingly, during his time as a house guest of Thomas Cranmer in 1549, Martin Bucer offered a critique of the emerging *BCP* liturgy. With respects to the Marriage Service he makes the following comment:

> The address which stands at the beginning of this order is excellently godly and holy: nevertheless at about the end of it three causes for matrimony are enumerated, that is children, a remedy, and mutual help, and I should prefer that what is placed third among the causes for marriage might be in the first place, because it is first."[8]

The *BCP* ordering of "causes" has continued to be contentious, with later liturgies placing love and companionship higher up the order, although some have also argued that Cranmer never intended a ranking of importance here but rather was listing the God-intended purposes of marriage.

> ***Secondly, It was ordained for a remedy against sin, and to avoid fornication; that such persons as have not the gift of continency might marry, and keep themselves undefiled members of Christ's body.***

The service is quite clear that the only place acceptable for sexual activity is marriage, and that marriage, whilst not merely for the satisfaction of "carnal lusts", nevertheless is given to avoid fornication and provided by God for those who might not have the gift of singleness.

This is consistent with the Homily on "The State of Matrimony":

> It is instituted of God, to the intent that man and woman should live lawfully in perpetual friendship, to bring forth fruit, and to avoid fornication. By which means a good conscience might be preserved on both parties, in bridling the corrupt inclinations of the flesh within the limits of honesty: for God hath straight forbidden whoredom and uncleanness, and hath from time to time taken grievous punishment of this inordinate lust, as all stories and ages have declared.[9]

---

[8] Quoted in Stevenson, *Nuptial Blessings*, p 140.
[9] See, "An Homily of the State of Matrimony", in *The Homilies*, (Fearn, Scotland: Focus Christian Ministries Trust, 1552, 1986), p 348.

The homily continues to outline the purpose of marriage by mentioning the blessing and nurturing of children, the avoidance of sin and offence, and the spiritual benefits of prayer and mutual support.[10]

Returning to the text of the *BCP* service, we note that the "gift of continency" is, by some, thought particularly to jar to the modern ear. If the passions (lusts) in a man or woman are so strong, why should they not find a healthy outlet in any form of loving relationship? And what if those passions are for the same sex rather than the opposite sex? The marriage service reflects that the appropriate place for these passions is in marriage (as defined by this service). But some are given the gift of celibacy. Modern readers are not the first to struggle with this teaching, Matthew 19 records Jesus' disciples struggling with his words. Some people find these teachings hard, both in terms of the exclusiveness of marriage and in terms of the challenge of living a faithful life outside of marriage. Jesus' disciples responded to his teaching on divorce with the comment "If this is the situation between a husband and wife, it is better not to marry" (Matthew 19:10).

> Jesus replied "Not everyone can accept this word, but only those to whom it has been given. For there are eunuchs who were born that way, and there are eunuchs who have been made eunuchs by others – and there are those who choose to live like eunuchs for the sake of the kingdom of heaven. The one who can accept this should accept it" (Matthew 19:11ff.).

The word "eunuch" is used three times in vv11-12. First, there are "eunuchs who are born that way". The traditional interpretation deduces that such men were either incapable of marriage (through disfigurement or handicap, perhaps, or in some cases, self-inflicted injury) or refers to men who do not wish to marry for whatever reason. Secondly, "there are eunuchs who have been made eunuchs by others", in other words, those who have been castrated. Thirdly, "there are those who choose to live like eunuchs for the sake of the kingdom of heaven". This is a conscious choice of chastity, which Paul argues is a gift given to him (see 1 Corinthians 7:7). The "gift of continency" or "celibacy" is rarely spoken about in the 21st Century but it is clearly in the mind of the liturgists as they celebrate the gift of marriage.

---

[10]  *The Homilies*, p 348f.

The *BCP* language might be difficult for us to today (by using words such as continency, carnal lusts, fornication, etc....) but reaffirming a God-given gift of singleness for the Kingdom's sake is an important message for the contemporary church, and reaffirming marriage as the God-given place for sexual intimacy is appropriate and necessary.

> *Thirdly, It was ordained for the mutual society, help, and comfort that the one ought to have of the other, both in prosperity and adversity. Into which holy estate these two persons present come now to be joined.*

Here is an assumption about the goodness of marriage. There is "mutual society" primarily for the comfort and help of the couple but also, perhaps, a hint of the wider good for society as we know it now. The commitment one makes to the other is in time of plenty and want (further amplified in the vows which husband and wife make to each other).

> *Therefore if any man can shew any just cause, why they may not lawfully be joined together, let him now speak, or else hereafter for ever hold his peace.*

> *I require and charge you both, as ye will answer at the dreadful day of judgement when the secrets of all hearts shall be disclosed, that if either of you know any impediment, why ye may not be lawfully joined together in Matrimony, ye do now confess it. For be ye well assured, that so many as are coupled together otherwise than God's Word doth allow are not joined together by God; neither is their Matrimony lawful.*

The congregation is invited to show any legitimate reason for the marriage not to take place if such a cause exists. The couple too are invited to disclose any reason why they may not lawfully be married and warned that failure to do so will be known by God and invalidate the marriage in his sight.

Marriage is only to be undertaken by mutual consent. Consent was assumed to be 14 for boys and 12 for girls, although usually marriage occurred into the 20's.[11]

---

[11] For a valid marriage to take place, both partners were required to have reached the age of consent—14 for boys and 12 for girls. A few marriages were solemnized at something near this age, but the vast majority of brides and grooms married later. The average age of marriage varied somewhat depending on location and social class, with marriages in the aristocracy taking place on average at about age 19 to 21 for women and age 24 to 26 for men, with occasional instances of much earlier marriage. But for most classes, the usual age was higher. Numerous studies confirm that the average age of marriage in England through most of the 1500s and 1600s was about 25 or 26 for women and 27 or 28 for men. See Young, *Family Life* p 41.

Three "causes" for marriage are thus enumerated. The wording of these reasons for marriage is remarkably similar to Heinrich Bullinger's 1541 book, *The Christian State of Matrimony*:

> Wedloke is the yoking together of one man and one woman whom God hath coupled together according to his worde with the consent of them both, from thenceforth to dwell together and to spend their life in an equall partakynge of all such things as God sendeth to the intent that they may bring forth children in the feare of him, that they may avoid whoredom, and that (according to God's good pleasure) the one may helpe and comfort the other.[12]

> *N, wilt thou have this woman to be thy wedded wife, to live together after God's ordinance in the holy estate of Matrimony? Wilt thou love her, comfort her, honour, and keep her in sickness and in health; and, forsaking all other, keep thee only unto her, so long as ye both shall live? The Man shall answer, I will.*

Both the man and the woman are invited to declare their willing consent one to another, promising to live together in holy matrimony. There is mutuality to their commitment one to another and, in this form of a covenant, the promise is not binding until both parties have pledged to each other.

The husband is asked to love, comfort, honour, keep her (in sickness and health); forsaking all others till death parts them. The assumption seems to be that only death can dissolve the marriage. The standard of love is high! And he is called to affirm "I will".

Philip Jensen makes the helpful point that the love to which they are called is one of a promise of fidelity. "Its unity is made by God and maintained by each party being faithful to the promises of their common agreement or covenant. Faithfulness rather than love lies at the basis of this union." [13] Such a standard of love is largely lost in a contemporary world where it is thought of entirely in romantic terms, and the feeling of "being in love" is what drives people to marry. Whereas the Puritans might have asked: "is this someone who you can learn to love", the modern age tends to ask: "do you feel love for this person". "Till death us do part" has become "till we fall out of love".

---

[12]   Quoted in Packer, *Among God's Giants*, p 344.
[13]   http://phillipjensen.com/articles/the-devolution-of-marriage/#sthash.3OpNtsZd.dpuf

*N. Wilt thou have this man to thy wedded husband, to live together after God's ordinance in the holy estate of Matrimony? Wilt thou obey him, and serve him, love, honour, and keep him in sickness and in health; and, forsaking all other, keep thee only unto him, so long as ye both shall live?*

*The Woman shall answer, I will.*

The preamble is similar but the promise she makes is to obey, serve, love, honour, keep, forsake...

This wording proves contentious for many modern couples and (as will be demonstrated below) later liturgies allow for the removal of "obey".

It should also be noted that if Ephesians 5 is being used as the basis of the vows the word is generally translated as "submit". Children "obey" (Ephesians 6:1); Wives "submit". The word is *hupotassómenoi* (inferred from the context of 5:21). This word implies that the wife is intended voluntarily to defer to her husband, which is rather different from the unquestioning obedience expected of children. Although we note that in 1 Peter 3:1, the motivation for obedience is for the salvation of the unbelieving husband, see further below.[14]

Modern services have largely removed this complementary language and have also removed references to the differently worded commitments for the man and the woman, expressed in the BCP language, leaving them as optional.

*I N. take thee N. to my wedded wife, to have and to hold from this day forward, for better for worse, for richer for poorer, in sickness and in health, to love and to cherish, till death us do part, according to God's holy ordinance; and thereto I plight thee my troth.*

Both husband and wife "take" each other, this is symbolised through the taking of each other's hands (explained in the rubric) as the vows are spoken. Each part of this promise is important:

- "To have and to hold", to take now, and to hold on to till the end;

- "For better for worse", when it is easy and when it is hard;

---

[14] Also the Homily outlines the positive benefits of a marriage which follows Peter's advice, see, "An Homily of the State of Matrimony", p.350.

- "For richer for poorer", in times of plenty, financial security and in times when money is tight;

- "Till death us do part", hinting again at the indissolubility of the relationship which can only be undone by death.

*I N. take thee N. to my wedded husband, to have and to hold from this day forward, for better for worse, for richer for poorer, in sickness and in health, to love, cherish and to obey, till death us do part, according to God's holy ordinance; and thereto I plight thee my troth.*

The promise the bride makes back to her groom is similar, although the bride includes the words "obey".

They both promise that their word to each other is "binding" and that they have made to each other truthful (troth) statements which they intend to keep.

*With this ring I thee wed, with my body I thee worship, and with all my worldly goods I thee endow: In the Name of the Father, and of the Son, and of the Holy Ghost. Amen.*

They loose hands and she receives a ring (in *ASB/CW* provision is made for both to receive rings), pledging it as a token: "with my body I thee worship". The ring does not make the marriage, but it does imply a covenantal commitment one to another in the sight of God.

Worship here, as elsewhere in the *BCP* is "giving worth" rather than idolising.

*Eternal God, Creator and Preserver of all mankind, Giver of all spiritual grace, the Author of everlasting life: Send thy blessing upon these thy servants, this man and this woman, whom we bless in thy Name; that, as Isaac and Rebecca lived faithfully together, so these persons may surely perform and keep the vow and covenant betwixt them made, (whereof this Ring given and received is a token and pledge,) and may ever remain in perfect love and peace together, and live according to thy laws; through Jesus Christ our Lord. Amen.*

It is curious that Cranmer points to Isaac and Rebecca as models of married life for the newly wed couple. She is shown to be a schemer who tricked her husband (Genesis 26:7; 27:11ff) and their behaviour does not appear to be held up by the Bible as exemplary. Nevertheless, it could be that Cranmer is more narrowly calling to mind that Rebecca is revealed as one who sought out the Lord (25:22), who was beautiful (26:7) and was loved by Isaac (24:66). Abraham and Sarah, who are referred to in a later prayer, are of course not an exemplary model of faithfulness (Genesis 20:2). The couple are blessed, or rather, the Priest asks God to bless them, for Cranmer did not understand the Priest to be administering a sacrament.

*Minister joins their right hands and says: "Those whom God hath joined together let no man put asunder" –*

Thus the act of marriage in some way binds them to each other. God has joined them together in an indissoluble union. Such teaching may be inferred from the passage we have already quoted, Matthew 19:4-6:

"Haven't you read," Jesus replied, "that at the beginning the Creator 'made them male and female,' and said, 'For this reason a man will leave his father and mother and be united to his wife, and the two will become one flesh'? So they are no longer two, but one. Therefore what God has joined together, let man not separate."

It is not only their pledge of faithfulness to each other which binds them (common hopes and aspirations in any marriage) but the affirmation that those who are joined together according to God's design for marriage cannot be "unmarried" or "decoupled". By quoting Matthew 19:6 Cranmer seems to believe that no human being can dissolve the marriage.

*Forasmuch as N. and N. have consented together in holy wedlock, and have witnessed the same before God and this company, and thereto have given and pledged their troth either to other, and have declared the same by giving and receiving of a Ring, and by joining of hands; I pronounce that they be Man and Wife together, In the Name of the Father, and of the Son, and of the Holy Ghost. Amen.*

The Minster speaks to the congregation: N & N have consented to each other, before God and before the congregation – therefore "I pronounce that they be Man and Wife together..." The minister is authorised to "pronounce them" married, insofar as by the act of declaring them duly married according to God's promise, they are now married.

The basis of marriage is summarised here as:

- Mutual consent;
- Witness before God and in his presence;
- Mutual declaration;
- Pledging with ring(s) given and received;
- Pronouncement of marriage.

Then follow various prayers:

First, a prayer of blessing that the couple may follow the example of Abraham and Sarah: the latter, in 1 Peter, is given as an example of the obedient wife. Then follows prayer for fruitfulness in childbearing (not if past childbearing age) and that the children would be brought up "Christianly and virtuously". The liturgy includes a prayer that their marriage would reflect the mystery of Christ and the Church (echoing Ephesians 5):

> *O God, who by thy mighty power hast made all things of nothing; who also (after other things set in order) didst appoint, that out of man (created after thine own image and similitude) woman should take her beginning; and knitting them together, didst teach that it should never be lawful to put asunder those whom you by Matrimony hadst made one : O God, who hast consecrated the state of Matrimony to such an excellent mystery, that in it is signified and represented the spiritual marriage and unity betwixt Christ and his Church; look mercifully upon these thy servants, that both this man may love his wife, according to thy Word, (As Christ did love his spouse the Church, who gave himself for it, loving and cherishing it even as his own flesh,) and also that this woman may be loving and amiable, faithful and obedient to her husband and in all quietness, sobriety and peace, be a follower of holy and godly matrons. O Lord, bless them both, and grant them to inherit thy everlasting kingdom; through Jesus Christ our Lord. Amen.*

This prayer summarises the key changes in the Protestant liturgy and prayers, namely that the husband and wife would signify and represent the spiritual marriage and unity between Christ and the Church. Even if the rest of the *BCP* service is superseded by other liturgies, it would be a shame to lose this central prayer, and it would be good to reintroduce it to all marriage services!

The final prayer is for God's blessing and grace upon the marriage.

> *God the Father, God the Son, God the Holy Ghost, bless, preserve, and keep you; the Lord mercifully with his favour look upon you; and so fill you with all spiritual benediction and grace, that ye may so live together in this life, that in the world to come ye may have life everlasting. Amen.*

Through the gift of marriage Christians are enabled to grow as believers, maturing in their Christian life and journeying towards everlasting life. Marriage, whilst not a sacrament, is also not merely a human institution. Marriage is given by God to grow the man and woman into Christ's likeness.

### Alternative to the Sermon

*All ye that are married, or that intend to take the holy estate of Matrimony upon you, hear what the holy Scripture doth say as touching the duty of husbands towards their wives, and wives towards their husbands.*

*Saint Paul, in his Epistle to the Ephesians, the fifth Chapter, doth give this commandment to all married men; Husbands, love your wives as Christ also loved the Church and gave himself for it, that he might sanctify and cleanse it with the washing of water, by the Word; that he might present it to himself a glorious Church, not having spot, or wrinkle, or any such thing; but that it should be holy, and without blemish. So ought men to love their wives as their own bodies. He that loveth his wife loveth himself: for no man ever yet hated his own flesh, but nourisheth and cherisheth it, even as the Lord the Church: for we are members of his body, of his flesh, and of his bones. For this cause shall a man leave his father and mother, and shall be joined unto his wife and the two shall be one flesh. This is a great mystery; but I speak concerning Christ and the Church. Nevertheless, let everyone of you in particular so love his wife, even as himself.*

*Likewise the same Saint Paul, writing to the Colossians, speaketh thus to all men that are married; Husbands, love your wives, and be not bitter against them.*

*Hear also what Saint Peter, the Apostle of Christ, who was himself a married man, saith unto them that are married; Ye husbands, dwell with your wives according to knowledge; giving honour unto the wife, as unto the weaker vessel, and as being heirs together of the grace of life, that your prayers be not hindered.*

*Hitherto ye have heard the duty of the husband toward the wife. Now likewise, ye wives, hear and learn your duties toward your husbands, even as it is plainly set forth in holy Scripture.*

*Saint Paul, in the aforenamed Epistle to the Ephesians, teacheth you thus; Wives submit yourselves unto your own husbands, as unto the Lord. For the husband is the head of the wife, even as Christ is the head of the Church; and he is the Saviour of the body. Therefore as the Church is subject unto Christ, so let the wives be to their own husbands in everything. And again he saith, Let the wife see that she reverence her husband.*

*And in his Epistle to the Colossians, Saint Paul giveth you this short lesson; Wives, submit yourselves unto your own husbands, as it is fit in the Lord.*

*Saint Peter also doth instruct you very well, thus saying; ye wives, be in subjection to your own husbands; that, if any obey not the Word, they also may without the Word be won by the conversation of their wives; while they behold your chaste conversation coupled with fear. Whose adorning, let it not be that outward adorning of plaited hair, and of wearing of gold, or of putting on of apparel but let it be the hidden man of the heart, in that which is not corruptible; even the ornament of a meek and quiet spirit, which is in the sight of God of great price, For after this manner in the old time the holy women also, who trusted in God, adorned themselves being in subjection until their own husbands; even as Sarah obeyed Abraham, calling him lord; whose daughters ye are as long as ye do well, and are not afraid with any amazement.*

The sermon consists of a biblical theology of marriage looking at the key texts which have shaped the wording of the liturgy.

The order of the treatment of the texts follows the order previously set out in the liturgy. We shall not spend much time on this sermon because, rather like the *Book of Homilies*, much of the text includes a retelling of the biblical passages.[15]

### 5.1.1    First to the husband

Ephesians 5 begins with the husband's responsibility to love the wife as Christ loved the Church.

Similarly, in Colossians, husbands are to love their wives and not be bitter with them.

In 1 Peter, the husband is to "dwell with" the wife, honour her, and treat her as the weaker vessel

### 5.1.2    Secondly, to the wife

Ephesians, then Colossians, both speak of the requirement of the wife to submit to her husband as to the Lord.

1 Peter uses a different word, translated here as "subjection". The wife's subjection to the husband is in order to win him over, without words, modelling her life on Sarah's obedience to Abraham.

---

[15]    See, "An Homily of the State of Matrimony", in *The Homilies,*

# 6 Subsequent liturgies

## 6.1 Book of Common Prayer/Alternative Service Book/Common Worship[1]

| BCP | ASB | CW |
|---|---|---|
| *Dearly beloved, we are gathered together here in the sight of God, and in the face of this congregation, to join together this Man and this Woman in holy Matrimony;* | *We have come together in the presence of God, to witness the marriage of N and N, to ask his blessing on them, and to share in their joy. Our Lord Jesus Christ was himself a guest at a wedding in Cana of Galilee, and through his Spirit he is with us now.* | *In the Presence of God, Father, Son and Holy Spirit we have come together to witness the marriage of N and N, to pray for God's blessing on them, to share their joy and to celebrate their love.* |
| *which is an honourable estate, instituted of God in the time of man's innocency, signifying unto us the mystical union that is betwixt Christ and his Church; which holy estate Christ adorned and beautified with his presence and first miracle that he wrought, in Cana of Galilee; and is commended of Saint Paul to be honourable among all men:* | *The Scriptures teach that marriage is a gift of God in creation and means of his grace, a holy mystery in which man and woman become one flesh. It is God's purpose that, as husband and wife give themselves to each other in love throughout their lives, they shall be united in that love as Christ is united with his Church.* | *Marriage is a gift of God in creation through which husband and wife may know the grace of God. It is given that as man and woman grow together in love and trust, they shall be united with one another in heart, body and mind, as Christ is united with his bride, the Church.* |
| *and therefore is not by any to be enterprised, nor* | *Marriage is given, that husband and wife may* | *The gift of marriage brings husband and wife* |

---

[1] The *Book of Common Prayer*, (Oxford: Oxford University Press, 1662); *The Alternative Service Book*, (London: SPCK, 1980); *Common Worship*, (London: Church House Publication, 2000).

| | | |
|---|---|---|
| taken in hand, unadvisedly, lightly, or wantonly, to satisfy men's carnal lusts and appetites, like brute beasts that have no understanding; but reverently, discreetly, advisedly, soberly, and in the fear of God; duly considering the causes for which Matrimony was ordained. | comfort and help each other, living faithfully together in need and in plenty, in sorrow and in joy. It is given that, with delight and tenderness they may know each other in love, and, through the joy of their bodily union, may strengthen the union of their hearts and lives. It is given, that they may have children and be blessed in caring for them and bringing them up in accordance with God's will, to his praise and glory. | together in the delight and tenderness of sexual union and joyful commitment to the end of their lives. It is given as the foundation of family life in which children are [born and] nurtured and in which each member of the family, in good times and in band, may find strength, companionship and comfort. And grow to maturity in love. |
| First, It was ordained for the procreation of children, to be brought up in the fear and nurture of the Lord, and to the praise of his holy Name. Secondly, It was ordained for a remedy against sin, and to avoid fornication; that such persons as have not the gift of continency might marry, and keep themselves undefiled members of Christ's body. Thirdly, It was ordained for the mutual society, help, and comfort that the one ought to have of the other, both in prosperity and adversity. | In marriage husband and wife belong to each other, and they begin a new life together in the community. It is a way of life that all should honour; and it must not be undertaken carelessly, lightly, Or selfishly, but reverently, responsibly, and after serious thought. | Marriage is a way of life made holy by God, and blessed by the presence of our Lord Jesus Christ with those celebrating a wedding at Cana in Galilee. Marriage is a sign of unity and loyalty which all should uphold and honour. It enriches society and strengthens community. No one should enter into it lightly or selfishly but reverently and responsibly in the sight of almighty God. |

| | | |
|---|---|---|
| Into which holy estate these two persons present come now to be joined. | This is the way of live, created and hallowed by God, that N and N are now to begin. They will each give their consent to the other; they will join hands and exchange solemn vows, and in token of this they will give and receive a ring. | N and N are now to enter this way of live. They will each give their consent to the other and make solemn vows, and in token of this they will [each] give and receive a ring. We pray with them that they Holy Spirit will guide and strengthen them. That they may fulfil God's purposes for the whole of their earthly life together. |
| Therefore if any man can shew any just cause, why they may not lawfully be joined together, let him now speak, or else hereafter for ever hold his peace. I require and charge you both, as ye will answer at the dreadful day of judgement when the secrets of all hearts shall be disclosed, that if either of you know any impediment, why ye may not be lawfully joined together in Matrimony, ye do now confess it. For be ye well assured, that so many as are coupled together otherwise than God's Word doth allow are not joined together by God; neither is their Matrimony lawful. | Therefore, on this their wedding day we pray with them, that. Strengthened and guided by God, they may fulfil his purpose for the whole of their earthly life together. But first I am required to ask anyone present who knows a reason why these persons may not lawfully marry, to declare it now. | First I am required to ask anyone present who knows a reason why these persons may not lawfully marry, to declare it now. |

## 6.2 Observations of similarities and differences between the three marriage services

All three services mention Christ's presence at Cana but the *Alternative Service Book (ASB)* and *Common Worship (CW)* have a more celebratory tone, emphasising the "grace of marriage".

### 6.2.1 Children

The first reason for marriage, in the *BCP*, in procreation. This is mentioned in the *ASB* and *CW* but not primary (in the latter it is also acknowledged that the marriage might take place with children already born).

### 6.2.2 Sinful relationships

The second reason for marriage in the *BCP* is as a remedy against sin/fornication which does not appear in later liturgies. With the acknowledgement in *CW* that children may already be present, plus widespread expectation that couples will have co-habited prior to marriage, the *BCP* language might be thought to be unrealistic by some today.

Of course, the Sarum right would have assumed Holy Communion to be included in the Marriage (and *BCP* may have this assumption too). The liturgy of the Holy Communion service would begin with Confession. It is noteworthy that *CW* makes provision for a dedication service following a civil marriage. This includes the prayer:

> **Lord our God, in our sin we have avoided your call. Our love for you is like a morning cloud, like the dew that goes away early. Have mercy on us; deliver us from judgement; bind up our wounds and revive us; in Jesus Christ our Lord.**

The absolution might include the following words:

> **The Lord forgive you your sin, unite you in the love which took Christ to the cross, and bring you in the Spirit to His wedding feast in heaven.**

The *CW* service enables a combination of celebration and confession, giving a helpful recognition of the complex backgrounds which many couples bring to the marriage. Cohabitation is now very common, and confessing failure and short comings in previous relationships should be encouraged (although strictly speaking this aspect is not part of the standard Marriage Service in any of the liturgies and only included in the dedication service following a Civil Marriage).

## 6.2.3    Social and mutual benefit

The third reason for marriage in the *BCP* is mutual society and comfort. All three services lay emphasis on the mutual benefit of marriage as well as the societal/communal benefit.

The "giving away" by the bride's father no longer features in modern marriage liturgies and the word "obey" in the bride's promise is given as an alternative (in the *ASB*) or placed in another part of the *CW* service booklet all-together. "Giving away" is thought to be too tied up with the transference of property and payment of dowries. In modern marriage, for the most part, couples come into the partnership as mature and independent adults, with their own financial security. Some such couples argue that "giving away" seems quaint but not very relevant, hence it is optional in later liturgies.

At the exchange of rings the words "with my body I thee worship" (*BCP*) are replaced by "with my body I honour you" (*ASB/CW*). "Worship" in this context, in 16th Century usage, had the sense of "giving something/someone their worth", the latter changes help clarify this. In the 1928 marriage service (and all subsequent liturgies) the vows are made symmetrical. The emphasis is on the equality of the partners rather than on their complementarity. Nevertheless, the option of complementary vows was reintroduced in the *ASB* under pressure from conservative voices wishing for the Pauline language to shape the liturgy.

Andrew Burnham makes the point that the liturgies reflect "Stages of a journey", with the possibility of seeing "the calling of the banns, the declarations, the vows, the giving of rings, the nuptial blessing, the registration of the marriage and the intercessions" in some way analogous to the linear progression of the mighty acts of "creation, redemption and the hope of salvation".[2] Some of the changes in the liturgy therefore reflect changes in society and church. For example, the journey from the home to the Church door (where, in the Sarum rite, some of the service took place) then on to the Church itself was reflected in the 16th century liturgies. The general thrust of "Gathering, Transformation and Mission" is helpful, although there will be

---

[2]    A. Burnham in S. Lake, *Using Common Worship Marriage* (London: Church House Publishing, 2000).

differences over exactly what "Transformation" is thought to have taken place in the *BCP* marriage service if it is assumed not to be a sacrament.

Charles Read has drawn on anthropologist Van Gennep's idea of "phased rites". Some of these are public (obviously the marriage, but also perhaps the engagement and subsequent wedding reception celebrations) and others are private (family meals, anniversaries etc.). Changes in the liturgy have in part reflected changes in societal attitudes towards public/private life. For example, given the prevalence of cohabitation prior to marriage, the public ceremony becomes more important, marking the attestation of love and commitment before family and friends.[3]

In sum, *Common Worship* concludes a series of revisions which have a more celebratory tone and with a greater sense of the whole gathered community taking part in the celebration.

Before we draw our thoughts to a conclusion it is worth a brief consideration of the 2013 Church House publication *Men and Women in Marriage*. This document was produced by the Faith and Order Commission (with agreement from the House of Bishops) and appeared at a very similar time to the Pilling Report. Perhaps because the former was overshadowed by the latter, *Men and Women in Marriage* has received very little public attention.

As a summary of the Church of England's understanding of marriage, it is successful. It reaches its appreciation of marriage from the *Book of Common Prayer*, Canon B30 and *Common Worship*. Marriage is described as being a "creation ordinance", it is defined in creation by God's good design as one man and one woman, and this is believed to be good for the "stability and health of human society" as well as

---

[3] I am not intending to get into any more detail on pastoral practice related to cohabitation, rather I am acknowledging that the decision to cohabit is made privately, thus the marriage ceremony, at a minimum, makes much of the public declaration. Gary Jenkins has written helpfully about this subject in *Cohabitation: a Biblical Perspective* (Bramcote: Grove Ethical Studies, No 84). It is also worth pointing out new research which has documented the likelihood of the success of marriage being tied to delay in sexual activity, ideally till after the day of marriage. Such research provides some compelling reasons for clergy to be involved in pre-marital teaching on the benefit of living according to the expectation of biblical marriage, well in advance of the actual preparation for the marriage service. See http://winteryknight.wordpress.com/2014/08/15/new-study-couples-that-delay-sexual-activity-experience-higher-quality-relationships/.

providing the best context for raising children. Whilst we may wish to say *more* in the modern context, I suggest that we should not say less![4]

The report raises a few issues related to the *BCP* understanding of marriage. First, the relationship between parenthood and partnership is explored:

> ... it is now the principle of union between one man and one woman that requires close attention. When we marry, we commit the procreative power of our own sex to an exclusive relation with a life-partner of the opposite sex. We open ourselves to parenthood in and through the partnership we enjoy as a couple, and that may be true even of a couple who, for whatever reasons, have no prospect of actually having children.[5]

It seems to me that this document rightly places the *BCP* emphasis on marriage as the place for procreation and childrearing whilst remaining sensitive to couples for whom there is little prospect of having children. The report also acknowledges that less ideal family units (that is, other than two biological parents raising their children) can provide good homes for children, but that this acknowledgment does not negate the secure place offered within the marriage bond.[6]

Secondly, the report helpfully engages with the three causes of marriage. St Augustine affirmed the three ends of marriage as being: offspring, faithfulness and sacramental union – not as "ends" but rather as "blessings that belong to marriage". Further:

> They were conceived originally as reflecting in some sense the spiritual growth of a marriage couple in the course of life: the physical good of the shared role in procreation laid the foundation for a moral responsibility towards each other, in turn allowing the union to attain a permanence which could speak to the world of God's own love. Taken together they describe the cultural bridge which marriage builds between the basic physical needs of our species and its spiritual vocation.[7]

---

[4]   *Men and Women in Marriage* (London: Church House Publishing, 2013), p 1ff. quoting the 2005 Civil Partnership: A Pastoral Statement from the House of Bishops, available online at https://www.churchofengland.org/media-centre/news/2005/07/pr5605.aspx

[5]   *Men and Women in Marriage*, p.7

[6]   *Men and Women in Marriage*, p.8

[7]   *Men and Women in Marriage*, p 10f.

Thirdly, the report contains a helpful section on the role of the State in marriage in the recognition that not all who marry are Christians. It argues that "the Church guards a common traditional understanding of marriage as a human, not only a religious act".[8] Thus there is a need for some pastoral flexibility and recognition of "hard circumstances" which require pastoral wisdom.

The report concludes with two paragraphs which recognise the contentious nature of the theological assumptions of the *BCP* marriage service in a modern society which has approved Same Sex Marriage.

> The meaning of pastoral accommodations can be misunderstood, as though the Church were solving pastoral difficulties by redefining marriage from the ground up, which it cannot do. What it can do is devise accommodations for specific conditions, bearing witness in special ways to the abiding importance of the norm. Well-designed accommodations proclaim the form of life given by God's creative goodness and bring those in difficult positions into close approximation to it. They mark the point where teaching and pastoral care coincide.[9]

One the one hand, the report affirms "the norm" as being marriage as defined by God. This does mean (as paragraphs 46-48 recognise) that accommodation on the basis of people's complex circumstances needs to be made. For example, I have heard an African Bishop articulate his stance on polygamy as follows: choose one wife as your own and ensure you meet your moral and financial responsibilities to the others. To the extent that good pastoral accommodation should point to the desirability of the norm and allow something to happen in a broken world in such a way that the true foundation of marriage is not undermined, it seems to me that this is sensible counsel.

On the other hand, the phrase "pastoral accommodation" may well have left open possibilities of a form of marriage which is accommodated to various kinds of partnerships – perhaps amounting to a church sanctioned "quasi marriage". This trajectory causes considerable concern for many of us. Moreover there is evidence that many will interpret the term "pastoral accommodation" to allow accommodations which, far from commending the abiding significance

---

8   *Men and Women in Marriage*, p 14f., referencing *An Honourable Estate* (London: Church House Publishing, 1988), Par. 42.

9   *Men and Women in Marriage*, p 16, para 49.

of monogamous heterosexual marriage, allow that which would be abhorrent to Cranmer and his liturgy.

The final paragraph reads as follows:

> It has seemed to some that the disagreement over same-sex marriage is a disagreement over mere names. But names govern how we think, and how we think governs what we learn to appreciate. When marriage is spoken of unclearly or misleadingly, it distorts the way couples try to conduct their relationship and makes for frustration and disappointment. The reality of marriage between one man and one woman will not disappear as the result of any legislative change, for God has given this gift and it will remain part of our created human endowment. But the disciplines of living in it may become more difficult to acquire, and the path to fulfilment, in marriage and in other relationships, more difficult to find.[10]

This paragraph may be read as saying: "the state may define marriage in different terms as a result of the legalisation of Same Sex Marriage but that does not alter the reality of true marriage as between one man and one woman". To this extent we welcome all attempts to speak clearly and with a biblical leading, expecting married couples to conduct themselves in line with biblical priorities. This does not close the door on complex conversations about the status of marriage in a divided culture and society, but it does help establish some parameters for further conversations.

## 6.3  Questions raised by the BCP understanding of Marriage

Our examination of the liturgy for the Solemnization of Marriage has looked at the history of the *BCP* Marriage Service; we have examined the text and have compared it with later revisions. In the light of the biblical assumptions which underpin ancient and modern liturgy we should now be better placed to consider some further questions about marriage.

### 6.3.1  Children

The first reason given for marriage, in the *BCP*, is children. For some this opened a debate over whether couples past childrearing should even be permitted to be married. We have noted Martin Bucer's objections at

---

[10] *Men and Women in Marriage*, p.16, para 50

the time of writing the *BCP* services suggesting that Cranmer's ordering of the causes of marriage should be reconsidered. Moreover, Genesis 2 presents the woman as a suitable helper and companion. With respects to the former, this includes the mandate to fill the earth with further images of God (Genesis 1:26f.). With respects to the latter, the role of marriage as a living parable of Christ's relationship with the Church (the mystery of Ephesians 5:21ff), the husband and wife complementarily loving and submitting, seems by Paul to be the primary purpose of marriage.

I doubt that a clergy person would advise a couple of childbearing age to consider marriage if either partner made it a pre-requisite that they would not have children. There is an expectation that in a healthy marriage, as the couple are able, they will produce more images of God to fulfil the creation mandate. The correct place for this to happen is in Christian marriage. Nevertheless, later liturgies which bring a more celebratory tone to the marriage service seem to better reflect the teleological goal of marriage as assumed by Paul in Ephesians 5. Thus, the parabolic nature of marriage should be seen to be as least as important as childbearing, in my view. The complementary interaction between husband and wife give a living example and public display of Christ's relationship with the Church.

For sure, Marriage is to be the place for procreation and thus the reason for the placement of this as the first "cause for which Matrimony was ordained." But we have noted that Genesis 2:23f does not necessarily start with an assumption that child birth is essential in order for it to be a true marriage; rather the clear implication is that if there is marriage, here is the place where God assumes children will be brought up. Perhaps we should agree with Martin Bucer that the third cause for which marriage is given should be mentioned first, without losing sight of the inextricable link between marriage and the expectation of childrearing.

## 6.3.2   Chastity

The *BCP* order places as the second cause for marriage: "marriage as a remedy against sin, and to avoid fornication; that such persons ... might marry, and keep themselves undefiled members of Christ's body." The assumption here is that all sexual intercourse outside of marriage (fornication/adultery) is sin and that marriage is a means whereby partners may present themselves undefiled before God.

The emphasis is on the purity and avoidance of sexual sin. One might hope that the liturgy would have a more celebratory tone by commending the godly benefits of a chaste life. If it is true that modern liturgies have lost the need to warn congregations about sin, it might also be fair to say that older liturgies did not always celebrate the benefits of a godly lifestyle. Moreover, the delight of the Song of Songs and other godly biblical examples of joy and tenderness in marriage might better commend a healthy approach towards marriage.

### 6.3.3    Companionship

Marriage is to be for "mutual society, help, and comfort". In their partnership, the man and woman are to find their complementary counterpart. The 16th Century expectation is not that you marry because of romantic love (as assumed in every "Romcom" plot-line). Rather, you marry someone who you will grow to love. The emphasis in the mutual vows made one to another is that it is the *promise* made to each other that will sustain them through the complexity of life's circumstances. Or, as Baxter advised, marry one who is lovely (or, perhaps adorned with inward rather than merely outer beauty, see 1 Peter 3:f.) and, to whom you will commit to be faithful throughout your entire life.

This was beautifully expressed by Robertson McQuilkin in 2004 when he resigned as president of Columbia Bible College and Seminary, in South Carolina to look after his wife suffering from Alzheimer's:

> When the time came, the decision was firm. It took no great calculation. It was a matter of integrity. Had I not promised, 42 years before, "in sickness and in health . . . till death do us part"?

> This was no grim duty to which I stoically resigned, however. It was only fair. She had, after all, cared for me for almost four decades with marvellous devotion; now it was my turn. And such a partner she was! If I took care of her for 40 years, I would never be out of her debt.

> Resignation was painful; but the right path was not difficult to discern... It is all more than keeping promises and being fair, however. As I watch her brave descent into oblivion, Muriel is the joy of my life. Daily I discern new manifestations of the kind of person she is, the wife I always loved. I also see fresh manifestations of God's love – the God I long to love more fully.[11]

---

[11]  http://www.christianitytoday.com/ct/2004/februaryweb-only/2-9-11.0.html?paging=off

## 6.4 Some outstanding questions raised by the BCP Marriage Service

1) The theology of marriage found in the *BCP* marriage service leans heavily upon the Genesis 2:24 passage and its New Testament context in Ephesians. In particular, we summarised this as: The complementarity of the man and the woman in marriage (the husband loving her as Christ loved the Church; the woman obeying (submitting to) him as she would Christ). The understanding of marriage according to a covenantal framework (although this word is not used) is after the Protestant interpretation of the word mystery.

**Question:** Is it possible to envisage that the view of marriage which is expounded in the *BCP* (and we believe is reflective of the use of Genesis 2:24 in the New Testament) could be applied to same sex marriage today? Would it be possible for a same sex couple to manifest the parabolic/mystery nature of marriage?

2) This booklet has not sought directly to discuss the question of Same Sex Marriage. Two observations might be made on this subject: first, and most obviously, the procreative function of marriage is given prominence in the *BCP* service. Some would argue that the Protestant acceptance of contraception has already made a separation between the sexual act and the potential for procreation. However, I think that this misses the argument about the obvious potential for procreation in heterosexual marriage (in most cases). Secondly, it would be fair to say that allowing the *BCP* Marriage Service liturgy to include Same Sex Marriage would be anachronistic and something that would never have been on the mind of Cranmer. Whether this closes down the debate about using the *BCP* liturgy (and its successors) for Same Sex Matrimony is another topic.

**Question:** In the light of our exposition of the *BCP* Marriage Service there would seem to be little room to square this with a 21st Century view that Same Sex Marriage is equally acceptable in the sight of God. However, should teaching about modern marriage place a greater emphasis on a Christian understanding of marriage as the place for child birth and heterosexual marriage as the assumed normal place for childrearing?

3) The issue of consent is carefully considered in the *BCP* service where both partners in the marriage and the wider congregation are called to attest that there is no reason in law why they may

not marry.[12] The emphasis is on the publicly witnessed nature of the event with apparently no part of the service any longer taking place in the home.

**Question:** Given the mobility of a modern congregation and the likelihood that both partners are not from the town where they are to be wed, how do we ensure the public attestation of a marriage happens and how do we ensure that marriage is in the presence of and to some extent accountable to the community in which the couple are to live?

4) Contemporary marriage in the Church of England is still dominantly via the publication of Banns. Many have objected that using Banns as a means to attest to the legal appropriateness of couples marrying is outdated in the modern world. However, the alternatives (marriage by licence/special licence) gives the Minister less opportunity for contact with the couple prior to the marriage and it could be argued that strong encouragement to be present in Church for the reading of the Banns and other opportunities for marriage preparation afford significant prospects of ensuring a Christian approach to the marriage service.

**Question:** This question is related to 3). Should modern marriage abandon the publication of Banns given that they perform very little function today and other means might be used to attest to the appropriateness of the couple being married?

5) Later liturgies have made provision for confession at the beginning of the service in the light of the prevalence of co-habitation, divorce,[13] and sometimes children in the relationship before marriage.

---

[12] The issue of "kindred and affinity" in BCP was a live topic in the 16th Century, such as the new permissions which allowed a man to marry his deceased brother's wife. Part of the reasons for this discussion was to clarify the boundaries of familial marriage and put parameters on what might be acceptable limitations. The other main legal objection of course is bigamy.

[13] The issue of Divorce is a large and complex topic, beyond the scope of this booklet, though there is a brief excursus on the subject at p 52. Moreover, because of the assumption about indissolubility very little concession is made in the direction of divorce by the Reformers (particularly Cranmer).

**Question:** How can we ensure that Confession and Celebration are a continuing part of the Marriage Service, particularly given the complexities of modern living and post-Christian background of the prevailing culture? Should there be a revival of the celebration of Holy Communion in modern marriage services or perhaps some other act of confession at the start of the service?

6) Later liturgies also have a greater emphasis on the mutuality of the relationship without the necessity of the Bride being "given away" by the father.

**Question:** Is "giving away" a quaint custom which is no longer relevant given that dowries are not paid and property is no longer transferred?

7) I am quite cautious proposing the liturgy according to the *BCP* marriage service for a modern marriage service in 2014. This is partly because of the anachronistic language, partly because I have some sympathy with Martin Bucer that the order of the "causes" of marriage should be altered, partly because I like the celebratory tone (and opportunity for confession) of some of the modern liturgy, and partly because no couple has yet requested me to use the *BCP* Marriage Service. I believe that there are some flaws in the *BCP* Marriage Service, but so too are there in every other subsequent marriage liturgy. The Protestant tone of the *BCP* Marriage Service is welcome and the rich English language encapsulated in this liturgy is unsurpassed.

**Question:** Can we still say that the *BCP* Marriage Service is the official liturgy and doctrine of the Church of England given that it is largely not used?

# 7   Conclusion

We have noted the richness of the *BCP* Marriage Service. We have observed the societal changes which have been reflected in the liturgy by a move from the home to the body of the Church building. We have also noticed the deliberate departure from the Sarum rite, particularly reflected in the understanding of marriage to be a "mystery" which reveals God's soteriological purposes, but nevertheless it is not considered to be a sacrament.

We have also seen that some modern services adopt both a more positive and celebratory tone (in places) and offer opportunity for repentance. Modern services also include more "egalitarian" vows between husband and wife, emphasising their equal commitment and promise one to another.

Nevertheless, the BCP Marriage Service makes certain assumptions about marriage which jar with modern trends: marriage is viewed as an indissoluble union between one man and one woman for life. Marriage is assumed to be the context for raising children and for the essential good of society. And, whilst they stand before God as equals, the complementary vows call upon the wife to obey her husband. And for both, marriage is part of Christian discipleship lived before God and according to his word.

In answer to some of the questions raised above I believe that to lose the theology of the *BCP* Marriage Service is further to depart from a biblical understanding of this rite. Whilst some might argue that 1662 did not go far enough in revising the Sarum rite, it seems to me that it is rich with a biblical understanding of the unfolding of God's mystery in and through human marriage, so that the watching world will have a greater appreciation of God's saving plans through his Church and anticipate all the more eagerly the final marriage of Christ, the groom, to his spotless bride, the Church. Plus, whilst continuing to debate its priority, the *BCP* Marriage Service draws an absolute connection between childbirth and childrearing and its place within marriage.

On balance, I will continue to use the *BCP* Marriage Service to help couples prepare for marriage to help ground them in a biblical theology of marriage which is not only good for them, but good for society at large and glorifying to God. My hope is that someone will produce a liturgy which is fair to Cranmer's Protestant intentions and rewrite it in a way which celebrates marriage and enables God to be glorified in the Marriage Service.

## 8    Excursus - The relevance of Genesis 2:24 for the discussion of Divorce, Remarriage and Indissolubility

Whilst broader than the topic of this study on the *BCP* Marriage Service, a brief excursus on the matter of Divorce and Remarriage is important. The reader might like to follow-up up footnotes to explore this topic further.

The two references to Genesis 2:24 in the synoptic Gospels are parallel passages in which Jesus answers questions about divorce and remarriage. The Pharisees tried to get Jesus to side with either the stricter interpretation of Moses' grounds for adultery (the followers of Shammai) or the more liberal views espoused by the Hillel school. In either case, responds Jesus, divorce was never intended to be the outcome of marriage. The marriage bond should be unbreakable. Jesus is not drawn into the debate surrounding the grounds upon which the "glue of one flesh union" may be dissolved, but rather he speaks about the created intention of the marriage union. We can observe in the BCP liturgy for the Marriage Service that similar assumptions about what might be called the "indissolubility" of marriage are made ("till death us do part... those whom God has joined together let no man put asunder").

In 1 Corinthians 6 Paul is dealing with a church which has been particularly notorious in its sexual conduct. "Do you not know?" (v.15) is a phrase Paul used to imply that there are truths which they should, and probably do, know but they are not living up to.[1] Each individual member of the church is part of the body of Christ. Paul asks rhetorically: "Do you not know that he who unites himself with a prostitute is one with her in body?"

> A couple's becoming "one flesh", which entails sexual congress whatever else it may entail, is comparable to the bonding between Christ and believers. They become members, limbs of his body, just as a husband loving his wife loves his own body, his own self (Ephesians 5:28-30)... The implication is clear: the satisfying of sexual desires is not wrong, and marriage is its appointed setting.[2]

---

[1]    C.K Barrett, *First Epistle to the Corinthians,* (location: A & C Black, 1967), p 148.
[2]    D.F. Wright, "Sexuality; Sexual Ethics" in eds. G. F. Hawthorne, R. P. Martin and D. G. Reid, *Dictionary of Paul and his Letters* (Nottingham: IVP, 1993), pp 872f.

Ephesians 5:22-32 has demonstrated that the "one flesh" union of husband and wife is clearly more than a sexual one. As we have already noted, by uniting one's self temporarily to a prostitute the Corinthian uses "one flesh" language with his actions without any intention of permanency. Sexual union is intended as the consummation of mutual ownership of one spouse to the other (see 1 Corinthians 7:3f.). Moreover, by uniting physically with a prostitute, Paul says, you are inappropriately taking the body which belongs to the Lord and uniting it with a body which is not destined for the resurrection.

Both these New Testament references point to the fact that the physical union does not make the marriage, rather, the marriage is "consummated" in the one flesh union following the public joining ceremony. Nevertheless, joining together in sexual union outside of marriage makes a statement which is unworthy of the believer. After all, we belong to the Lord, and what we do with the body therefore matters.[3]

Divorce, then, might be permissible in certain circumstances. We note that the Continental and British Reformers diverge on this issue with Luther and Bucer arguing for a State sanctioned Divorce (for legitimate reasons, name adultery, see Matthew 22:23-33[4]) thus potentially allowing for the remarriage of the divorcee. Cranmer and other British Reformers were less persuaded by this argument and the *BCP* Marriage Liturgy shows great affinity with the prevalent Catholic notion of indissolubility. However, within the *BCP* Marriage Service, there are no hints that the marriage could or should be dissolved, and why would it? We should not expect anything other than a joyful celebration of the event in this or any other marriage liturgy. Wenham and Heth provide a fuller exploration of this topic in *Jesus and Divorce*.[5]

---

[3]   See Gordon Fee, *The First Epistle to the Corinthians* (Grand Rapids, Michigan: Eerdmans, 1991), p 260.

[4]   Jesus answers questions about the remarriage of a widow here, but note the assumption that upon dissolution remarriage is assumed.

[5]   Gordon Wenham & William Heth, *Jesus and Divorce*, (Carlisle: Paternoster Press, 1984, 2002).

# LATIMER PUBLICATIONS

# Latimer Publications

### Anglican Foundations Series

| | | |
|---|---|---|
| FWC | The Faith We Confess: An Exposition of the 39 Articles | Gerald Bray |
| AF02 | The 'Very Pure Word of God': The Book of Common Prayer as a Model of Biblical Liturgy | Peter Adam |
| AF03 | Dearly Beloved: Building God's People Through Morning and Evening Prayer | Mark Burkill |
| AF04 | Day by Day: The Rhythm of the Bible in the Book of Common Prayer | Benjamin Sargent |
| AF05 | The Supper: Cranmer and Communion | Nigel Scotland |
| AF06 | A Fruitful Exhortation: A Guide to the Homilies | Gerald Bray |
| AF07 | Instruction in the Way of the Lord: A Guide to the Prayer Book Catechism | Martin Davie |

### Latimer Books

| | | |
|---|---|---|
| GGC | God, Gays and the Church: Human Sexuality and Experience in Christian Thinking | eds. Lisa Nolland, Chris Sugden, Sarah Finch |
| WTL | The Way, the Truth and the Life: Theological Resources for a Pilgrimage to a Global Anglican Future | eds. Vinay Samuel, Chris Sugden, Sarah Finch |
| AEID | Anglican Evangelical Identity – Yesterday and Today | J.I.Packer, N.T.Wright |
| IB | The Anglican Evangelical Doctrine of Infant Baptism | John Stott, Alec Motyer |
| BF | Being Faithful: The Shape of Historic Anglicanism Today | Theological Resource Group of GAFCON |
| TPG | The True Profession of the Gospel: Augustus Toplady and Reclaiming our Reformed Foundations | Lee Gatiss |
| SG | Shadow Gospel: Rowan Williams and the Anglican Communion Crisis | Charles Raven |
| TTB | Translating the Bible: From Willliam Tyndale to King James | Gerald Bray |
| PWS | Pilgrims, Warriors, and Servants: Puritan Wisdom for Today's Church | ed. Lee Gatiss |
| PPA | Preachers, Pastors, and Ambassadors: Puritan Wisdom for Today's Church | ed. Lee Gatiss |
| CWP | The Church, Women Bishops and Provision: The Integrity of Orthodox Objections to the Proposed Legislation Allowing Women Bishops | |
| TSF | The Truth Shall Set You Free: Global Anglicans in the 21st Century | ed. Charles Raven |
| LMM | Launching Marsden's Mission: The Beginnings of the Church Missionary Society in New Zealand, viewed from New South Wales | eds. Peter G Bolt David B. Pettett |

*If you have enjoyed this book, you might like to consider*

- *supporting the work of the Latimer Trust*
- *reading more of our publications*
- *recommending them to others*

*See www.latimertrust.org for more information.*